ORADEA

TRAVEL GUIDE 2024

Discover Oradea's hidden gems and ancient wonders in 2024 edition

Jay Pittman

ORADEA TRAVEL GUIDE 2024

COPYRIGHT © 2023 BY JAY PITTMAN

Reserved rights apply. Without the publisher's prior written consent, no portion of this publication may be copied, distributed, or transmitted in any way, including by photocopying, recording, or other mechanical or electronic means, with the exception of brief quotations used in critical reviews and other noncommercial uses allowed by copyright law.

ORADEA TRAVEL GUIDE 2024

TABLE OF CONTENTS

CHAPTER ONE: INTRODUCTION

CHAPTER TWO: GETTING STARTED

CHAPTER THREE: HISTORICAL LANDMARKS

CHAPTER FOUR: HIDDEN GEMS

CHAPTER FIVE: CULTURAL EXPERIENCES

CHAPTER SIX: OUTDOOR ADVENTURES

CHAPTER SEVEN: NIGHTLIFE AND ENTERTAINMENT

CHAPTER EIGHT: PRACTICAL INFORMATION

CHAPTER EIGHT: PRACTICAL INFORMATION

CHAPTER NINE: DAY TRIPS

CHAPTER TEN: CONCLUSION

CHAPTER ONE: INTRODUCTION

Welcome to Oradea

Oradea, a city rich in culture and history, extends a warm invitation for you to discover its charms. Oradea, which combines its rich history with modernity in a seamless manner, is a charming location located in northwest Romania, on the banks of the Crisul Repede River. You will be enthralled by the city as you go about it because of its architectural marvels, historical sites, and friendly locals.

Antiquated Tapestry

The history of Oradea is longstanding, with indications of human habitation in the region dating back to the Stone Age. The city has been impacted by many different civilizations throughout the ages, including Austrian, Ottoman, Hungarian, and Roman. The architecture, customs, and manner of life of the city all reflect this rich historical tapestry.

The city's Old Town, which has well-preserved structures from several eras, is a veritable gold mine of historical marvels. Oradea Fortress, a medieval stronghold dating back to the 12th century, is evidence of the city's tenacity in the face of several adversities throughout history. Wandering the cobblestone alleys and admiring the palaces built in the Baroque style, visitors may experience the ambiance of a bygone period.

Building Masterpieces
Oradea is well known for its many architectural styles, which include Art Nouveau, Secession, Gothic, and Baroque. The Black Eagle Palace, a magnificent specimen of Art Nouveau architecture,

is one of the city's crown jewels. For those who like architecture, the elaborate detailing on the front and the opulent interiors make it a must-visit location.

Wander around the city's center, Union Square, and you'll come across an amazing collection of architectural treasures. Awe-inspiring examples of the city's architectural wonders include the State Theatre and the Moon Church, with its distinctive astronomical clock.

Artistic Tapestry
Oradea is a thriving center of innovation and culture, not merely a place made of buildings. The city offers a look into its creative essence via its many museums, galleries, and cultural events. Housed in a splendid Baroque mansion, the Oradea Art Museum has a centuries-spanning collection of Romanian and European art.

Oradea accepts modern culture as well as traditional art with open arms. The city offers both residents and tourists a vibrant and interesting experience all year with its many cultural festivals, concerts, and events.

What's New in 2024 Edition
As 2024 approaches, Oradea keeps developing and innovating, giving its appeal new depths. This edition offers tourists a number of new innovations that will improve their entire experience of seeing this charming city.

1. Ecological Projects
Oradea is leading the way in environmentally friendly projects and sustainable practices, with a renewed emphasis on preserving the environment. The city is expanding its green areas and taking steps to lessen its carbon impact. In addition to seeing the city's dedication to a better future,

visitors may participate in eco-tours and investigate sustainable design.

2. Progress in Technology

Oradea is using modern technology to improve the experience for visitors in line with the times. Technology is being easily incorporated into smart city efforts and interactive guided tours with augmented reality capabilities to make exploring more entertaining and educational.

3. Appetizing Treats

Oradea's restaurant industry is experiencing a resurgence, with new cafés, restaurants, and diners providing a wide variety of delectable dishes. For those who love to eat, the city is a culinary paradise, offering both international and traditional Romanian cuisine. An innovative culinary festival honoring the marriage of classic tastes with modern twists is being introduced in the 2024 edition.

4. Programs for Cultural Exchange

Oradea is collaborating with towns all over the globe to promote cross-cultural contact. Through cultural events, exhibits, and performances that highlight the richness of worldwide creative expressions, this effort gives the city a touch of the world. Cross-cultural interactions allow visitors to form memories that cut beyond national boundaries.

5. Well-being and leisure

Oradea is increasing the range of wellness and leisure activities it offers, realizing the value of overall health. For those looking to unwind, new spas, health centers, and yoga retreats provide a peaceful haven. Oradea's natural surroundings, which include adjacent hot springs, enhance the healing experience and make it a place suitable for exploration as well as leisure.

Finally, Oradea extends an invitation for you to go on a sensory-rich, time-traveling adventure. Oradea has a lot to offer everyone, whether they are passionate about architecture, history, food, or just want to get away from it all and spend some time in the great outdoors. The 2024 edition opens a new chapter of advancement and innovation, guaranteeing that your trip to this historic city will be nothing short of spectacular.

CHAPTER TWO: GETTING STARTED

Oradea is a little city tucked in the western region of Romania that entices visitors with its fascinating history, gorgeous architecture, and lively culture. Whether you're an experienced traveler or a first-time visitor, this guide will provide you with the knowledge you need to make your time in Oradea unforgettable.

Travel Tips

1. Requirements for Entry:
Make sure your passport is up-to-date before you go to Oradea. Verify the visa requirements according to your country of citizenship and make sure all required paperwork is in order.

2. Banking and Currency:

The Romanian Leu (RON) is the official currency of Romania. For the best prices, it is advised to convert currencies at nearby banks. With their widespread distribution around the city, ATMs provide easy access to cash.

3. Vernacular:
Even though Romanian is the official language, English is widely spoken among Oradeans, particularly in the city's tourist regions. Acquiring a few fundamental Romanian words might improve your communication and experience.

4. Relative Courtesies:
Warm hospitality is a well-known trait among Romanians. It is polite to shake hands with strangers, look them in the eye while speaking, and arrive on time. In restaurants and taxis, tipping is customary and usually amounts to 10% of the total cost.

5. Climatic Conditions: The climate of Ordoña is temperate-continental. Warm summers are followed by sometimes snowy, chilly winters. Taking into account the season of your trip, pack appropriately.

6. Regional Food:
Savor the mouthwatering Romanian food. Sample some of the regional specialties, such as mici (grilled sausages), sarmale (cabbage rolls), and mămăligă (cornmeal porridge). Try your meals with some țuică, a traditional plum brandy, or with some local wines.

7. Security:
Oradea is usually seen as secure for tourists. But it's wise to use caution while handling personal items and to be alert in public settings.

Transportation

1. How to Get There: Through Air:

Oradea International Airport (OMR), which has flights to important European cities, is the closest international airport. As an alternative, you may fly into Budapest Ferenc Liszt International Airport (BUD) or Cluj-Napoca International Airport (CLJ), from which you can take a bus or rail to Oradea.

Via Train:
Oradea is a well-served railway station that receives trains from places around Europe. Beautiful vistas of Romania's landscape may be seen when traveling by rail.

Via Bus:
Numerous bus companies provide routes from nearby nations to Oradea. To ensure smooth travel, check timetables and purchase tickets in advance.

2. How to Get Around Oradea: Transportation by Public:

Oradea has a well-functioning bus and tram system for public transportation. Get your tickets straight from the driver or at kiosks. For longer visits, a rechargeable travel card is a more affordable choice.

Services for Taxis:
Taxis are affordable and widely accessible. Make sure the taxi is equipped with a meter, and settle on the fee in advance of the trip.

Riding a bike and strolling:
Oradea's downtown is easy to navigate on foot since it is designed with pedestrians in mind. One well-liked and environmentally beneficial way to see the city and its environs is by renting a bike.

3. Hospitality:
Oradea has a variety of lodging choices, ranging from opulent hotels to welcoming guesthouses. The thermal spa sector and the old city center are popular places to stay. It is advised to make

reservations in advance, particularly during the busiest travel times.

1. Activities and Attractions: The Fortress of Oradea:
Discover the remarkably preserved Oradea Fortress, a historically significant site with an intriguing fusion of architectural forms.

2. Eagle Palace Black:
Admire the Black Eagle Palace's magnificent Art Nouveau building, which houses the Oradea Art Museum.

3. Felix Baths:
Unwind at the Felix thermal baths, which are close to Oradea and are renowned for their therapeutic qualities.

4. Citadel Park:

Enjoy a leisurely walk in Citadel Park, a lovely green area that provides peace and quiet in the middle of the city.

5. Vacation Days:

Think about going on day excursions to some of the surrounding sites, such as the Apuseni Mountains, Băile Tușnad, or the quaint town of Bucium.

Final Thoughts

Oradea delivers a singular vacation experience with its distinct combination of natural beauty, history, and culture. You'll be ready to make the most of your visit to this fascinating Romanian location if you heed this travel advice and navigate the city's transit alternatives. Oradea has something for every kind of tourist, whether they are attracted to the city's architectural wonders, thermal spas, or gastronomy. Have fun on your travels!

CHAPTER THREE: HISTORICAL LANDMARKS

Oradea, a city rich in cultural and historical legacy, is home to a number of sites that serve as reminders of its intriguing history. Union Square, Black Eagle Palace, and Oradea Fortress are particularly important landmarks. Let's examine the specific historical and architectural aspects of each of these well-known locations.

Oradea Fortress

Background in History: Oradea Fortress, often referred to as Oradea Citadel or Oradea Stronghold, was founded in the eleventh century. Its roots may be found in the Hungarian Kingdom, during King Ladislaus I's reign over the area. Over the years, the castle was vital to the kingdom's defense against several invasions.

Architectural Features: The stronghold had many architectural makeovers, fusing different architectural philosophies that represent the wide range of cultural influences in the area. Built in the Romanesque style at first, it gradually included Gothic and Renaissance features. During the Ottoman Empire, the stronghold was further strengthened with defensive walls and bastions.

Notable Structures: The spectacular Keep Tower, a representation of Oradea's medieval defensive system, is open for exploration by guests inside the castle. The Moon Church, which is close to the stronghold, enhances its historical appeal with its distinctive astronomical clock and eye-catching architecture.

Restoration Efforts: To ensure that the Oradea Fortress's historical value is preserved across time, efforts have been undertaken to repair and preserve it in recent years. The goal of restoration work is to present the many architectural motifs that have influenced the fortress's development throughout the ages.

Black Eagle Palace

Architectural Gem: One of Oradea's most recognizable sites is the Black Eagle Palace, a magnificent example of Art Nouveau architecture. The palace, which was designed by the famous architect Ferenc Siklódy, was finished in 1908. Detailed sculptures, elaborate embellishments, and a dramatic black eagle statue that graces the façade are some of its distinguishing characteristics.

Historical Significance: Oradea's palace has seen important events in its cultural and economic history. It was first constructed as a bank headquarters. It represented the wealth and energy of the city's Belle Époque era and acted as a symbol of success throughout that period.

Architectural Elements: The palace's façade is decorated with Art Nouveau-style wrought-iron accents, sculpted figures, and floral patterns. The inside is just as stunning, with large hallways, windows made of stained glass, and ornate décor that takes guests back to a more opulent time in history.

Adaptive Reuse: The Black Eagle Palace has been converted into offices, retail spaces, and cultural organizations in the modern day. This flexible strategy guarantees that Oradea's architectural treasure will always be a dynamic aspect of the city.

Union Square

The Historical Center of Oradea: Union Square, also known as Piața Unirii, is the center of Oradea and a hub for historical, cultural, and social activities. The area, surrounded by vibrant baroque structures, has a distinct appeal that honors the city's varied past.

Architectural Ensemble: The Union Square neighborhood has a tasteful fusion of Neo-Classical, Rococo, and Baroque architectural elements. The Church with the Moon, the Greek Catholic Bishopric Palace, and the Oradea State Theater are a few notable structures.

Union Square is a shining example of Oradea's Baroque influence, which swept the city in the eighteenth century. Both residents and visitors are drawn to the gorgeous backdrop created by the complex sculptures, vivid colors, and baroque façade.

Events and Festivals: Throughout the year, the square is a lively location for a number of events and festivals. Union Square is a communal hub that unites people via events like open-air concerts and cultural festivities, promoting a feeling of pride and solidarity.

Final Thoughts

Oradea's historical sites, including Union Square, Black Eagle Palace, and Oradea Fortress, tell a story of the city's tenacity, variety, and architectural splendor. Oradea is a destination that skillfully blends history and modernity because of these monuments, which not only add to the city's dynamic present but also serve as memories of the past.

CHAPTER FOUR: HIDDEN GEMS

Oradea is a little city in western Romania that is well-known for its magnificent architecture and rich history, but it also has some undiscovered attractions that make it a wonderful travel destination for anyone looking for unusual experiences. On our tour, we will discover Oradea's hidden gardens, neighborhood cafés and restaurants, and handcrafted stores that give the city even more charm.

Secret Gardens

1. "The Garden of the Moon"
The Moon Garden is a peaceful, aesthetically pleasing hidden haven tucked away from the busy metropolis. The calm ambiance is created by its well-kept gardens, which are embellished with

sculptures and exotic flora. Wander around winding trails, take in the soothing murmur of fountains, and locate quiet areas for introspection.

2. The Castle

Though not completely concealed, people often miss Castle Park's lesser-known areas. Encircling the Oradea Fortress, this ancient park provides a charming environment complete with concealed seats, flower gardens, and old trees. It's the ideal location for spending a peaceful day away from the bustle of the city.

3. The Garden of Botany

An oasis of biodiversity, Oradea's Botanical Garden is a veritable hidden treasure for those who love the outdoors. It has a wide variety of plants in it, including rare and threatened species. The garden offers a tranquil and enlightening escape, offering an insight into the marvels of the plant world.

Local Cafés and Eateries

1. Art Café
Tucked away in a charming lane, Café D'Arte is a warm place that brings together passions for coffee and art. The artwork of regional artisans gives the café a distinctive feel. Coffee lovers and art aficionados will find paradise on the menu, which has an array of gourmet coffees and delicious pastries.

2. La Tavi
La Tavi is a family-run restaurant renowned for its real Romanian food and a hidden treasure for foodies. This restaurant has a cozy environment, tucked away from the major streets. The menu offers a flavor of the area's culinary history by showcasing classic meals made with fresh, locally sourced ingredients.

3. Oradea's Street Food Market

The street food market in Oradea is a must-visit for anybody looking to sample the regional cuisine in a more relaxed atmosphere. This undiscovered treasure appears in many places, with a diversified array of street food vendors serving a wide variety of cuisines. It's the ideal location to experience the city's thriving and delectable street food scene.

Artisanal Shops

1. Artisan's Retreat

Enter Craftsman's Haven, a secret shop that features the work of regional artists. This business is a gold mine of one-of-a-kind, distinctive things, with anything from handcrafted jewelry to finely designed home décor pieces. It gives guests the chance to purchase local handicrafts and bring home a little of Oradea's creative history.

2. Antique Jewels

This shop, which features a carefully chosen selection of vintage clothing, antique furniture, and unusual objects, is a hidden treasure for fans of the retro aesthetic. Because of the proprietors' excellent sense of style, the store is a refuge for those who value vintage charm. Discovering antique treasures is like setting off on a voyage across time.

3. The Corner of the Artisans

Handmade workmanship is celebrated in this little, charming corner store. A carefully chosen assortment of things made by regional craftsmen is gathered at The Artisan's Corner, ranging from leather goods to handwoven fabrics. In addition to buying one-of-a-kind goods, visitors can see the talent and attention to detail that go into each creation.

In conclusion, for those who are ready to go beyond the typical tourist sites, Oradea's hidden treasures provide a tapestry of experiences. Oradea welcomes you to experience the charm that is hidden from the usual road, whether you're looking for the peace of hidden gardens, the delectable tastes of neighborhood cafés, or the artistry of artisanal stores.

CHAPTER FIVE: CULTURAL EXPERIENCES

Oradea is a quaint city in northwest Romania that enthralls both residents and tourists with its diverse range of cultural activities. Oradea is a refuge for people looking to learn more about Romanian culture, from colorful festivals honoring the city's history to carefully chosen museums and galleries displaying its creative talent.

Oradea's Festivals

1. International Theater Festival of Oradea:
Every year, the Oradea International Theatre Festival turns the city into a platform for artistic performances. The festival offers a wide array of theatrical performances by both domestic and foreign troupes, creating a melting pot of different dramatic emotions. The festival fosters local talent

while encapsulating the spirit of world theater, including both avant-garde and traditional pieces.

2. Oradea hosts the Transylvanian International Film Festival (TIFF):
The Transylvanian International Film Festival, a continuation of the well-known TIFF in Cluj-Napoca, brings together movie buffs in Oradea. This cinematic spectacle encourages a passion for the seventh art among both inhabitants and visitors by bringing a carefully chosen collection of foreign and Romanian films to the city's screens.

3. Jazz Festival in Oradea:
Oradea's cobblestone streets come alive with music during the yearly Jazz Festival. This festival highlights the variety of jazz styles, from traditional to modern, and is hosted in scenic locations across the city. It adds to the region's cultural mix by

bringing jazz to a wider audience in addition to drawing in seasoned enthusiasts.

4. The Medieval Festival of Oradea:
During the Medieval Festival, Oradea's streets transform into a time portal to the Middle Ages, bringing the city's history to life. Attendees are transported to a bygone period via authentic costumes, historical reenactments, and traditional crafts, providing a unique window into the region's cultural past.

Museums and Galleries

1. The Art Museum of Oradea:
A veritable gold mine of European and Romanian art from several eras may be found in the Oradea Art Museum. The museum, which is housed in a magnificent Baroque castle, has decorative arts, paintings, and sculptures that provide visitors with

a thorough understanding of the development of creative expression in the area.

2. The Museum of the Criş Country, or Muzeul Ţării Crişurilor:

This museum offers an immersive experience via its exhibitions, delving into the local history and customs of the Criş area. From folk art to archeological discoveries, Oradea's different populations' cultures and lifestyles are shown to tourists.

3. The Museum Ady Endre:

This museum honors the life and contributions of Endre Ady, a well-known poet from Hungary and one of Oradea's literary greats. Manuscripts, private items, and interactive exhibits allow visitors to examine Ady's influence on the local cultural scene.

4. The 1989 Revolution Memorial Museum:

Oradea was a major player in the 1989 Romanian Revolution, and this museum honors the occasions that brought about the demise of communism. Through the use of multimedia displays, images, and eyewitness narratives, the museum offers a moving meditation on a crucial juncture in Romania's contemporary past.

Oradea's Cultural Fusion:
Oradea's cultural experiences are not confined to certain events or museums; rather, they are a part of everyday life and merge well with modern influences and customs. The city's combination of Neoclassical, Secessionist, and Baroque architectural styles provides witness to its historical development.

The atmosphere of cross-cultural interchange permeates Oradea's streets, even beyond the well-planned events and carefully decorated places. Customary marketplaces, where residents exchange handcrafted goods and local specialties, develop into focal points for communication between various groups. The gastronomic scene also reflects this dynamic interaction of cultures, with restaurants serving fusions of traditional Romanian foods with tastes from throughout the world.

In summary, Oradea's cultural offerings are a colorful patchwork that captures both the historical richness and the modern energy of the city. Oradea welcomes both locals and tourists to participate in a rich tapestry of cultural discovery, whether through the prism of festivals that honor creative expression or the carefully planned spaces of museums and galleries that protect and highlight history.

CHAPTER SIX: OUTDOOR ADVENTURES

Oradea is a quaint city in western Romania that is well-known for its abundance of outdoor activities in addition to its rich history and architectural treasures. We will look at three thrilling outdoor activities in this guide that highlight Oradea's natural beauty and leisure options.

Băile Felix Thermal Baths

A Summary and Location:
The Băile Felix Thermal Baths are a refuge of rest and renewal, just a short drive from Oradea. These thermal springs, which are tucked away in a gorgeous setting, have a long history. The Romans were the first to notice the therapeutic benefits of the thermal waters.

Events: Heated Pools: Băile Felix is well-known for its several hot pools, each with its own individual mineral makeup and temperature. Indulge in the healing properties of the warm waters while taking in the verdant surroundings.

Spa and Wellness Centers: In addition to saunas, massages, and mud baths, the thermal complex has other health and spa amenities. These facilities provide the ideal balance of recreational and health advantages.

Activities Outside: Outside of the swimming pools and spa services, Băile Felix provides outdoor leisure options. The area's natural beauty may be explored by tourists thanks to the walking paths around it.

Advise for Guests: Make sure you have enough towels and swimsuits.

Utilize the range of wellness services available for a whole sense of relaxation.

Verify the hours of operation as well as any special occasions or offers.

Crisul Repede River Walks

A Summary and Location:

For those looking for a more strenuous outdoor experience, the Crisul Repede River Walks provide a fantastic way to get in touch with the natural world. Oradea is home to the Crisul Repede River, whose banks provide both residents and visitors with beautiful strolling routes.

Events: Visual Tours: The river paths provide a calm environment for strolls. The trails are kept up well and travel along the sides of rivers, providing breathtaking views of the surrounding flora and water.

Cycling paths: Along the river, cyclists may enjoy designated cycling paths that provide a more active approach to taking in the area's natural beauty.

Observing Birds: For those who like birding, the riverbank setting is a great place to see a variety of bird species. You could get views of herons, ducks, and other waterfowl with binoculars and a sharp eye.

Advise for Guests: For the river hikes, wear suitable walking shoes.
If you want to explore more actively, think about hiring a bike.
Take a picnic and enjoy a leisurely lunch by the river.

Nymphaea Aquapark

A Summary and Location:

The exciting Nymphaea Aquapark in Oradea is a great place to go for water-based experiences. This aquapark has something for everyone, whether you're an adrenaline addict searching for water slides or a family looking for a pleasant day out.

Entertainment: Slides and Features: There are several different types of water slides at Nymphaea, ranging from kid-friendly ones to heart-pounding ones for the daring. Wave pools and lazy rivers are among the many attractions, guaranteeing an exciting day.

Play Areas for Kids: Specialized play areas with small pools, water fountains, and interactive elements are available to families with young children, providing a fun and safe atmosphere.

Comfort Zones: Nymphaea offers areas with loungers and jacuzzis for leisure, enabling guests to unwind in the vibrant ambiance of the water park for a more relaxed experience.

Advise for Guests: Verify the age and height limitations for certain rides.

To get the most out of your day at the aquapark, arrive early.

Wear sunscreen and drink plenty of water, particularly on hot days.

Results

Oradea offers the ideal combination of adventure and relaxation with its wide range of outdoor activities. This Romanian city has something for everyone, whether your preference is to explore riverfront paths, take a dip in hot springs, or experience the exhilaration of a water park. As you go out on your outdoor activities in Oradea, remember to savor the beauty of the natural world and the unique pleasures this little place has to offer.

CHAPTER SEVEN: NIGHTLIFE AND ENTERTAINMENT

Oradea, a city in western Romania, has a thriving nightlife scene that accommodates a wide variety of preferences and inclinations. After dusk, the city comes alive with a variety of entertainment choices for those in search of it, ranging from hip clubs and pubs to exciting live music venues.

Bars and Pubs

Oradea is home to a large number of pubs and taverns, each with its own atmosphere and menu. The city has something for everyone, whether you're searching for a quiet place to sip a craft brew or a bustling location for drinks and dancing.

1. Irish pub The Dubliner:

The Dubliner is a well-known Irish bar that draws both residents and visitors to Oradea. It is situated right in the city center. With its traditional Irish décor, live music, and extensive beer list, which includes Irish stouts and ales, the pub has a cozy, welcoming vibe.

2. Mica Bella:
Bella Muzica is a must-visit for everyone who enjoys a historic environment. This elegantly refurbished 18th-century structure that houses the pub has a laid-back vibe while maintaining grandeur. There is a wide selection of quality spirits and cocktails for patrons to savor.

3. In the Town:
Down Town is a chic, younger-oriented pub that's perfect if you're feeling quite modern. This facility is ideal for an evening of dancing and mingling because of its contemporary décor, DJ performances, and extensive drink menu.

4. Eagle Black:

Black Eagle provides a warm environment with exposed brick walls and subdued lighting for a more personal encounter. With a bottle of wine or a specialty drink mixed by talented mixologists, it's a perfect spot to relax.

5. Blues & Jazz Club:

Jazz fans will like the Jazz & Blues Club, which has a refined but relaxed vibe thanks to live performances. Music enthusiasts frequent the bar because it often showcases jazz acts from across the world and locally.

Live Music Venues

Oradea has a thriving live music scene with a variety of venues showcasing anything from jazz and electronic music to pop and rock. Here are a few notable locations for live music:

1. Café Moszkva:

For many years, the famous Moszkva Café has been a mainstay of Oradea's music scene. It presents live events with bands from across the world and locally that play anything from indie to rock and alternative.

2. Monday Blues:

For lovers of rock and blues, this place is a sanctuary. Music fans may enjoy soulful sounds and excellent conversation in an intimate environment at Blue Monday, which often hosts live performances by skilled artists.

3. Music Club Mandala:

Mandala is a vibrant music venue that welcomes a wide range of patrons. Mandala provides a vibrant environment for individuals who appreciate dancing and exploring new sounds, with live rock bands and DJs spinning electronic music.

4. History Club:

The Old Times Club, housed in a historic structure, adds a vintage touch to the live music scene. The location often showcases acoustic concerts, giving the audience a cozy and engaging experience.

5. The Fabrica Club:

Live music concerts are a frequent fixture at Club Fabrica, one of Oradea's best venues for nightlife. Renowned for its vibrant ambiance, the venue draws in both domestic and foreign performers for remarkable shows.

To sum up, Oradea's nightlife and entertainment scene provide a diverse range of experiences, ranging from classic Irish pubs to cutting-edge dance clubs and from iconic live music venues to trendy hotspots.

CHAPTER EIGHT: PRACTICAL INFORMATION

Oradea, a little city in northwest Romania, provides a unique combination of contemporary energy and historical depth. For a smooth stay in Oradea, whether you're a business traveler attending a conference or a leisure visitor looking for a cultural experience, you need to know some basic facts about lodging, food, and helpful connections.

Accommodations

Oradea offers a wide range of lodging choices, from upscale hotels to more affordable ones. Here are a few noteworthy selections:

1. Hilton Oradea DoubleTree: This luxurious hotel, which is in the heart of the city, has large rooms, contemporary conveniences, and a soothing spa. For business travelers or those looking for a little more luxury, it's a great option.

2. Contemporary Hotel Continental Forum Oradea: This hotel, which blends beauty and utility, is located next to the Black Hawk Palace Arcade. Its well-equipped meeting rooms make it appropriate for business gatherings, while for leisure tourists, its close proximity to other attractions is a bonus.

3. Ramada Oradea: A mid-range choice including cozy accommodations and a number of amenities, such as an on-site restaurant and fitness facility. It's at a handy location for those on work or vacation.

4. The Empire of Pensions: Take a look at this lovely guesthouse if you want something more personal. It offers a flavor of the hospitality found in the area with its warm environment and individual service.

5. Cost-effective hostels: Travelers on a tight budget may check out hostels like Oradea Hostel for a reasonably priced stay that doesn't sacrifice basic facilities or hygiene.

Local Cuisine

Oradea offers a fantastic gastronomic experience that combines regional influences with classic Romanian delicacies. The following local cuisines are a must-try:

1. Polenta with brânză și smântână (sauce and sour cream): This dish, a mainstay of Romanian cooking, is made of porridge made from cornmeal that is liberally topped with sour cream and local cheese.

2. Sarmale (Cabbage Rolls): filled cabbage leaves with rice, spices, and minced beef; often served over polenta. The deep tastes of home cuisine in Romania are reflected in this meal.

3. Grilled sausages, or miccios: Usually, a combination of pig, beef, and lamb is used to make these little seasoned sausages. Perfectly grilled, they go well with fresh bread and mustard.

4. Papanași: Fried or boiled dumplings stuffed with sweet cheese and garnished with sour cream and fruit jam make up this delectable delicacy.

5. ^uică: A well-liked regional spirit, Șuică is Romania's traditional plum brandy. It is often served with traditional foods or as an aperitif.

Useful Contacts
Having all of your important connections close at hand guarantees a seamless stay in Oradea. Here are a few helpful contacts:

1. Emergency Services: Emergency Number: 112—for prompt help in the event of an emergency, catastrophe, or other emergency.

2. Local Transportation: Oradea Public Transport: +40 359 800 829 - Details on public transport timetables and routes.

3. Tourist Information Center: Oradea Tourist Information: +40 259 432 936: Offers help with maps, pamphlets, and basic information about the attractions in the city.

4. Airport Details: Oradea International Airport: +40 259 416 077 for details on flights, airport amenities, and ways to get around.

5. Embassy/Consulate: Your country's embassy in Romania: Having your embassy or consulate's contact information on hand is crucial in case of emergencies or needing diplomatic assistance.

To sum up, Oradea's useful information guarantees a happy and relaxing stay. The city is welcome with open arms, offering a wide range of lodging alternatives, delicious local food, and valuable connections. Oradea's unique mix of modernism and history makes for a memorable visit, whether you're here on business or for pleasure.

CHAPTER NINE: DAY TRIPS

Explore Surrounding Areas

Oradea is a little city in northwest Romania that is well-known for its stunning architecture and rich historical background. It also acts as a starting point for exploring the surrounding regions. Day tours from Oradea reveal a rich tapestry of varied landscapes, cultural landmarks, and scenic beauties. We'll explore some of the most alluring day excursions from Oradea in this guide; each one offers a unique combination of adventure, history, and leisure.

1. Hunyadi Castle and Deva Citadel (around two hours by car) Start your trip by traveling southeast to the medieval city of Deva. Situated atop a volcanic hill, the Deva Citadel provides expansive views of the surrounding area. Discover the 13th-century fortress's remarkable preservation and the strategic significance it has had throughout history. The architectural wonder of Hunyadi Castle, one of the most important medieval structures in Transylvania, is located not far from the citadel. Explore the Knight's Hall, take in the Gothic-Renaissance architectural combination, and learn about the castle's lore, which includes the fabled well with its amazing 30-meter depth.

2. The Thermal Baths in Baile Felix (about 20 minutes by car) Visit Baile Felix, one of Romania's most well-known spa resorts, for a tranquil day. Savor the healing thermal pools and baths supplied by organic thermal springs. The resort's contemporary amenities provide the ideal fusion of peace and well-being. In the middle of verdant foliage and tranquil settings, rejuvenate your body and mind.

3. The Scărișoara Ice Cave and Bears Cave (about three hours by car)

Go west to the Apuseni Mountains to see the wonders of nature. Renamed after the many bear bones discovered inside, the Bears Cave has amazing stalactite and stalagmite structures. Guided tours provide unique insights into the geology and history of the cave. Proceed towards the Scărișoara Ice Cave, which harbors one of Europe's biggest subsurface glaciers. Discover the ice formations' remarkable features and the cave's own environment. Traveling through the Apuseni Mountains offers breathtaking views and an insight into rural life.

4. Pădurea Craiului Mountains and Suncuius (around 1.5 hours by car) Suncuius, a charming town at the base of the Pădurea Craiului Mountains, is a haven for nature lovers. Hike along paths that lead to breathtaking vistas and weave through lush woodlands. Apuseni National Park is a sanctuary for hikers and wildlife lovers alike because of its wide variety of flora and animals.

55

5. Arad-Arches City (about an hour's drive) Arad is easily reached by car in the northeast; the city is renowned for its striking architecture and lively arts and culture scene. Wander around the city center, which is filled with opulent Baroque structures and recognizable arches. Discover the history of the city by seeing the 18th-century fortress known as Arad Fortress and perusing the exhibits at the nearby museums.

6. Hungary's Hortobágy National Park and Salonta (around 1.5 hours by car) Venture into Hungary and explore the Hortobágy National Park, sometimes known as the "Puszta." Discover the wide plains, the distinctive flora and animals of this UNESCO World Heritage site, and traditional Hungarian horse displays. The surrounding village of Salonta provides a quaint window into Hungarian history and culture.

7. Satu Mare and the Maramureş Wooden Churches (approximately 2 hours by car) Head north to the historically significant city of Satu Mare. Take a walk along the charming riverbank, explore the city center, and pay a visit to the Satu Mare County Museum. Continue to Mămăureş, which is well-known for its wooden churches that are on the **UNESCO** World Heritage List. Learn about the distinctive architectural design and rich cultural history of these fascinating buildings.

Recap: Oradea's advantageous position makes it possible to do a wide range of day trips, from visiting neighboring nations and ancient citadels to relaxing spas and breathtaking natural formations. Oradea's surroundings provide a variety of experiences, including leisure, outdoor activities, and cultural immersion. Your tour of this fascinating area will be further enhanced by the unique experiences that each day excursion offers. With careful planning, you may find the undiscovered treasures that Oradea offers as a starting point for a wide range of fascinating adventures.

CHAPTER TEN: CONCLUSION

Summary and Farewell

Oradea is a quaint city in northwest Romania that has a thriving environment, a broad range of cultures, and a long history. As we approach the end of our investigation of Oradea, it is appropriate to provide a thorough synopsis and say a heartfelt goodbye to the distinctive features that make this city so special.

Historical Overview: There is evidence of human habitation in Odarata as far back as the Stone Age. The region has a long history. It saw the control of many empires throughout the ages and saw considerable changes. This historical tapestry is reflected in the city's architecture, which has elements from the Ottoman Empire, the

Austro-Hungarian Empire, and other historical periods.

Architectural Marvels: The city's rich architectural history is one of its most distinctive features. Oradea's strategic significance throughout history is shown by the medieval fortress known as the Oradea Fortress. The two main attractions are Union Square, which has structures in the Baroque style, and the Black Eagle Palace, a magnificent example of Art Nouveau architecture. Discovering the city is like entering a live history book since every structure has a unique tale to tell.

Cultural Tapestry: The identity of Oradea is shaped by influences from Romania, Hungary, Germany, and Judah, making it a melting pot of cultures. The city's theaters, festivals, and museums all showcase how rich its cultural heritage is. The Ady Endre Museum and the Museum of the Crisana Region both provide insights into the history and literary legacy of the area. Oradea's creative vitality and cultural variety are celebrated throughout its festivals, which include the Oradea Music Days and the Medieval Festival.

Thermal Springs and Wellness: Oradea is well known for its thermal springs, which provide both residents and tourists with a chance to unwind and revitalize. A peaceful haven is offered by the Felix Baths, a combination of thermal pools and spa services. Oradea is a popular destination for visitors looking for both cultural experiences and health because of the healing properties of the mineral-rich waters, which have drawn people for centuries.

Gastronomic Delights: A city's tour isn't complete unless its gastronomic options are sampled. Oradea's cuisine, which combines classic German, Hungarian, and Romanian tastes, is a reflection of its cosmopolitan heritage. Local markets, like Oradea Central Market, provide traditional specialties and fresh goods. The city's food culture is a fascinating trip for the senses, offering everything from sweet pastries to robust stews.

Education and Innovation: Oradea is a center for innovation and education in addition to being a city rich in history and culture. The academic quality of Oradea University adds to the intellectual life of the city. Oradea's dedication to advancement and growth is shown by the establishment of research institutions and innovation hubs.

Sustainable programs: Oradea has embraced sustainability programs in the last several years, emphasizing green areas, eco-friendly procedures, and environmentally conscious urban design. The city's dedication to sustainability is a reflection of its progressive mindset, guaranteeing that urban growth and the natural world live together.

Prospects for the Future: It is clear from our investigation of Oradea that it is well-positioned for a vibrant future. Oradea is in a good position to draw tourists and maintain a high standard of living for its citizens because of its solid foundation in history, culture, education, and sustainability. Oradea's enduring attraction will be bolstered by further urban development initiatives and a dedication to conserving its cultural legacy.

Farewell to Oradea: No one excursion could ever include all of this city's nuances; therefore, it is difficult to say goodbye to Oradea. For those who are lucky enough to see it, the interwoven strands of history, culture, architecture, and invention form a tapestry that will never fade. May the memories of Oradea stay with us as a constant reminder of the beauty that results when tradition and modernity converge.

In conclusion, Oradea is more than just a city; it is a living tapestry of narratives, with every structure and cobblestone evoking a different time in history. Oradea provides a varied and rewarding experience for everyone, whether they are looking for the peace and quiet of thermal springs, the thrill of cultural events, or the cerebral stimulation of scholarly endeavors. By the time our trip to Oradea comes to a close, we have gained a greater appreciation of a city that skillfully combines its rich past with a vision for the future, in addition to photos and mementos.

Printed in Great Britain
by Amazon